my name is tijuana.

Introduction

Tijuana and his mom made his journal and wanted to share what's working for them. His plan really helps him do his sight words even though it is still hard.

They think you'll like doing a journal too. You can use it for practicing sight words or math facts or stopping screen time or brushing your teeth or even doing homework. And lots more!

You can use Tijuana's journal to get ideas of what you want your journal to say.

You can write it yourself, like Tijuana did, or you can ask someone else to write for you while you think of what to say. You can even add your own drawings like he did, if you want.

Send us an email about your journal and how it helped you grow your brain. Can't wait to see!
Send your journal sample to info@thebadgesofpower.com.

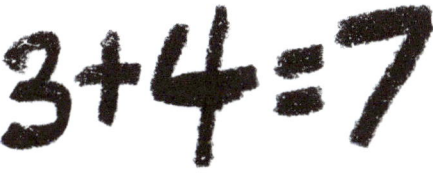

3+4=7

Cover design and illustrations by Joe Bauman

Book Production by Miramare Ponte Press LLC
www.miramarepontepress.com

Hardback ISBN: 979-8-9885059-5-2
Paperback ISBN: 979-8-9885059-6-9

Arkwright, Nan
Tijuana's Journal / Nan Arkwright
Tijuana's Journal is a personal space for young adventurers to document their strategies, successes, and growth while conquering challenges. This accompanying journal to Tijuana Mañana, the Anxious Iguana encourages creativity and determination as kids embrace their own paths to success.
ISBN: 979-8-9885059-5-2

DEDICATIONS

Nan:
To families, educators, therapists and other carers
looking for ways to co-regulate with their child
when doing something that feels like 'too much.'

Joe:
To my wife and kids, for inspiring and supporting
me in all of my artistic pursuits. And as always, to
God for providing me another opportunity to
glorify Him through my art.
And of course my pups!

REVIEWS

Tijuana Iguana, and the accompanying journal, empower children to recognize and self-manage their "big feelings." Parents also discover effective approaches to help these children. Written and illustrated in a gentle, light-hearted fashion, these books would work for children from preschool through elementary school. Tijuana's Journal provides a semi-structured way for children to describe their feelings, and then develop their own solutions for management. I highly recommend these books for children (and their parents) struggling with "big feelings."

- Deborah A. Sedberry MD
Behavioral and Developmental Pediatrician

I like the Tijuana story line and the attached journal that kids can use to make their own plan. It seems practical and will help the adult reading the story know how to translate the lesson to whatever is hard for their child.

- Becky V., Elementary School Principal

I love that there's a journal that accompanies Tijuana Mañana the Anxious Iguana so kids can make their own plans for working on their sight words - or anything they think is hard to do. I can't wait to look at the resources Nan provides on her website that will further reinforce messages in her book and journal.

- Andra Harris
Barton tutor, Mom of a child with dyslexia, and author of Magnificent Meg

I just love this book so much! I can imagine a teacher reading it to a class and it creating such empathy for kids who struggle, as well as generating a way for the kids who are struggling to describe what's going on. The illustrations are so well done. The companion journal adds a hands-on opportunity to actually apply in daily life messages learned from the book.

Dr. Liz Angoff, Licensed Educational Psychologist, ExplainingBrains.com (http://explainingbrains.com/)

Tijuana's Journal (Written with my mom) Yay!

me (arrow pointing to "Ti" in Tijuana)

What Tijuana knows:

When I feel like <u>reading</u> is "Too Much" I can work together with <u>my mom</u>. 🖤💜

<u>She</u> will listen to my Big Feelings and will share <u>her</u> calm with me so I feel safe.

Even when I'm having a hard time with my Big Feelings, <u>She</u> will be there to help.

We can even do something together to help because we have a plan.

We could <u>count together</u> or <u>take Buster for a walk</u>.

1-2-3-4

That will help me feel a little less upset because <u>She</u> is helping me.

And it will help my Upstairs Brain talk to my Downstairs Brain. Plus, the stairs between them will get stronger from practicing. I will get used to practicing and learning new things.

<u>My mom</u> and I can play games to help me focus when I'm practicing.

Following the plan <u>my mom</u> and I make will help me feel more confident. ☺

I'm ready to be <u>Tijuana Today</u>! 🐷

_____**Journal** (Written with my _____)

What _____ knows:

When I feel like _____ is "Too Much" I can work together with

_____.

_____ will listen to my Big Feelings and will share _____ calm with me so I feel safe.

Even when I'm having a hard time with my Big Feelings, _____ will be there to help.

We can even do something together to help because we have a plan.

We could _____ or _____.

That will help me feel a little less upset because _____ is helping me.

And it will help my Upstairs Brain talk to my Downstairs Brain.

Plus, the stairs between them will get stronger from practicing.

I will get used to practicing and learning new things.

_____ and I can play games to help me focus when I'm practicing.

Following the plan _____ and I make will help me feel more confident.

I'm ready to be _____!

Tijuana's Plan for Reading Sight Words:

How will an adult know you need a little help with your Big Feelings?

When I hide under my blanket.

Where do you think you will feel those Big Feelings in your body?

I might feel a little stuck in my brain, like I can't think.

What thoughts do you think you might have?

Like it's "Too Much" and that I don't want to be in trouble.

How would you like an adult to remind your Downstairs Brain that there's not really an emergency?

Make a song for counting to 100 by tens.

(10-20-30-40-50-60-70-80-90-100!)

What would help your Downstairs Brain to start hearing your Upstairs Brain so they can start working together?

I think walking Buster together since I think that my "Downstairs Brain" would pay attention to how cute he is.

I ♥ Buster! →

When your Upstairs Brain and your Downstairs Brain start working together, what messages do you think will encourage you to practice your reading so the staircase will get stronger?

I don't have to know everything about reading yet. Practicing will help me learn more.

_____ <u>Plan for Reading Sight Words:</u>

How will an adult know you need a little help with your Big Feelings?

_____

Where do you think you will feel those Big Feelings in your body?

_____

What thoughts do you think you might have?

_____

How would you like an adult to remind your Downstairs Brain that there's not really an emergency?

_____

What would help your Downstairs Brain to start hearing your Upstairs Brain so they can start working together?

_____

When your Upstairs Brain and your Downstairs Brain start working together, what messages do you think will encourage you to practice your reading so the staircase will get stronger?

_____

What tools will you and an adult use to help your Upstairs Brain focus?

Hmmm. I think maybe playing a Memory game with the sight words would be fun.

Do you think following this plan will be easy or hard?

At first, I think it will be hard, but maybe after my birthday, it will start to feel easier.

Do you think you will be able to follow the plan?

Yes but at first, with my mom doing it with me until I feel more confident to do it alone.

What feeling do you think you'll have each time you practice?

I think I will feel encouraged and proud that my brain is growing.

What will be helpful to remember when it is time to practice together again tomorrow?

Um, just do it and then when PopPop comes to visit, I can show him what I have learned! And then he will know why my new name is Tijuana Today!

What tools will you and an adult use to help your Upstairs Brain focus?

_____

Do you think following this plan will be easy or hard?

_____

Do you think you will be able to follow the plan?

_____

What feeling do you think you'll have each time you practice?

_____

What will be helpful to remember when it is time to practice together again tomorrow?

_____

My Journal About

_____

_____ **Journal** (Written with my _____)

What _____ knows:

When I feel like _____ is "Too Much" I can work together with

_____.

_____ will listen to my Big Feelings and will share _____ calm with

me so I feel safe.

Even when I'm having a hard time with my Big Feelings, _____ will be

there to help.

We can even do something together to help because we have a

plan.

We could _____ or _____.

That will help me feel a little less upset because _____ is

helping me.

And it will help my Upstairs Brain talk to my Downstairs Brain.

Plus, the stairs between them will get stronger from practicing.

I will get used to practicing and learning new things.

_____ and I can play games to help me focus when I'm

practicing.

Following the plan _____ and I make will help me feel more

confident.

I'm ready to be _____!

_____ Plan for Reading. _____ :

How will an adult know you need a little help with your Big Feelings?

_____

Where do you think you will feel those Big Feelings in your body?

_____

What thoughts do you think you might have?

_____

How would you like an adult to remind your Downstairs Brain that there's not really an emergency?

_____

What would help your Downstairs Brain to start hearing your Upstairs Brain so they can start working together?

_____

When your Upstairs Brain and your Downstairs Brain start working together, what messages do you think will encourage you to practice your reading so the staircase will get stronger?

_____

What tools will you and an adult use to help your Upstairs Brain focus?

_____

Do you think following this plan will be easy or hard?

_____

Do you think you will be able to follow the plan?

_____

What feeling do you think you'll have each time you practice?

_____

What will be helpful to remember when it is time to practice together again tomorrow?

_____

My Journal About

_____

_____Journal (Written with my _____)

What _____ knows:

When I feel like _____ is "Too Much" I can work together with

_____.

_____ will listen to my Big Feelings and will share _____ calm with

me so I feel safe.

Even when I'm having a hard time with my Big Feelings, _____ will be

there to help.

We can even do something together to help because we have a

plan.

We could _____ or _____.

That will help me feel a little less upset because _____ is

helping me.

And it will help my Upstairs Brain talk to my Downstairs Brain.

Plus, the stairs between them will get stronger from practicing.

I will get used to practicing and learning new things.

_____ and I can play games to help me focus when I'm

practicing.

Following the plan _____ and I make will help me feel more

confident.

I'm ready to be _____!

_____ Plan for Reading. _____ :

How will an adult know you need a little help with your Big Feelings?

_____

Where do you think you will feel those Big Feelings in your body?

_____

What thoughts do you think you might have?

_____

How would you like an adult to remind your Downstairs Brain that there's not really an emergency?

_____

What would help your Downstairs Brain to start hearing your Upstairs Brain so they can start working together?

_____

When your Upstairs Brain and your Downstairs Brain start working together, what messages do you think will encourage you to practice your reading so the staircase will get stronger?

_____

What tools will you and an adult use to help your Upstairs Brain focus?

_____

Do you think following this plan will be easy or hard?

_____

Do you think you will be able to follow the plan?

_____

What feeling do you think you'll have each time you practice?

_____

What will be helpful to remember when it is time to practice together again tomorrow?

_____

My Journal About

_____

_____**Journal** (Written with my _____)

What _____ knows:

When I feel like _____ is "Too Much" I can work together with

_____.

_____ will listen to my Big Feelings and will share _____ calm with

me so I feel safe.

Even when I'm having a hard time with my Big Feelings, _____ will be

there to help.

We can even do something together to help because we have a

plan.

We could _____ or _____.

That will help me feel a little less upset because _____ is

helping me.

And it will help my Upstairs Brain talk to my Downstairs Brain.

Plus, the stairs between them will get stronger from practicing.

I will get used to practicing and learning new things.

_____ and I can play games to help me focus when I'm

practicing.

Following the plan _____ and I make will help me feel more

confident.

I'm ready to be _____!

<u>_____</u> Plan for Reading. <u>_____</u> :

How will an adult know you need a little help with your Big Feelings?

_____

Where do you think you will feel those Big Feelings in your body?

_____

What thoughts do you think you might have?

_____

How would you like an adult to remind your Downstairs Brain that there's not really an emergency?

_____

What would help your Downstairs Brain to start hearing your Upstairs Brain so they can start working together?

_____

When your Upstairs Brain and your Downstairs Brain start working together, what messages do you think will encourage you to practice your reading so the staircase will get stronger?

_____

What tools will you and an adult use to help your Upstairs Brain focus?

_____

Do you think following this plan will be easy or hard?

_____

Do you think you will be able to follow the plan?

_____

What feeling do you think you'll have each time you practice?

_____

What will be helpful to remember when it is time to practice together again tomorrow?

_____

ABOUT THE AUTHOR

As a pediatric occupational therapist, Nan sees many children who struggle with learning. Unfortunately, some may think they are 'bad' or 'dumb.' Nan wrote this book to help them understand how the brain works so they can re-frame their thinking and see themselves as kids who care and want to learn and can, with gentle guidance from an adult who slows down and meets them where they are.

To reinforce the bold messages of a healthy mindset and developing self-awareness, she has created *Tijuana's Journal* where he and his mom create a plan for what to do when something feels like 'too much.' You can order your own journal at:
http://www.ahopskipandajumpahead.com/books

Nan went to the Galapagos in Ecuador and enjoyed learning about the iguanas that live there.

Did you know?

Some iguanas can hold their breath 60 seconds.
Mockingbirds let out a distinctive call when there is a Galapagos Hawk in the area and the iguanas then run for cover.
Iguanas sneeze saltwater out their nose.

Nan thought an iguana would be a good character for this story because they run, hide, or act aggressive when their brains think there is an emergency. (Remember what Tijuana did when his brain told him reading was an emergency?)

Kids do that sometimes too. But, as they grow, they learn that most problems are not emergencies. This means their reactions are usually much smaller because they can think about how to solve problems and do hard things, just like Tijuana was practicing.

ABOUT THE ILLUSTRATOR

Joe Bauman is a self-taught multimedia artist and illustrator based in Danville, CA. Joe's interest in drawing began at a very early age. He would draw characters from cartoons, old movies, and superhero comic books. Godzilla and Spider-Man were his favorite characters to draw.

Joe is working on a variety of creative book projects so from this point forward, he'll be at his desk, drinking lots of coffee, listening to music, talking to his dog Frankie, and creating new drawings and stories for you to enjoy.

Get out your pencil and start building a plan for your brain. Just follow these 3 steps:

1. Visit our website, www.ahopskipandajumpahead.com/books.
2. Start the conversation about how to build strong steps between the Upstairs and Downstairs Brains by using these fun activities with the child in your life.
3. Scan the QR code and leave a review on Amazon.

Mental Health Children's Books on Social - Emotional Regulation

Check out more social - emotional regulation books about animals from The Galapagos collection.

Mindful Seymour Pauses - a series on thinking before you don't think. Collect them all!

Tijuana Mañana the Anxious Iguana - on what's going on in Tijuana's brain to make him dance with excitement and believe in himself, even though he's scared of sight words.

Tijuana's Journal, the companion to *Tijuana Mañana the Anxious Iguana* - on finding your own way to dance with excitement and believe in yourself.

Check out more social - emotional regulation books in The Prosocial Behaviors collection.

Lions and Worries and Safety, Oh My! A Social-Emotional Learning Adventure on the Serengeti - on turning worrisome social situations into feelings of safety, with a little help from the strong and mighty herd of elephants who leaves no one behind.

(A one-of-a-kind reading experience integrating educational technology into this interactive chapter book.)

Check out more social - emotional regulation books in The Emotional Regulation collection.

No, Kito, No! - a series on feeling respected, supported, accepted and valued thanks to kind friends who help an adorable giraffe turn No, Kito, No! into Yes, Kito, Yes!

Expect the Unexpected! Choco Learns About Emotional Regulation - on handling all kinds of emotions when things don't go the starfish's way.

What Could Be Going On? Inigo Learns About Emotional Regulation - on understanding others' intentions by talking it out and expecting the best from them.

Check out the first social - emotional regulation book.

Mission: CONTROL! A Big Feelings Adventure! - on doing hard things, even when it feels like "too much."

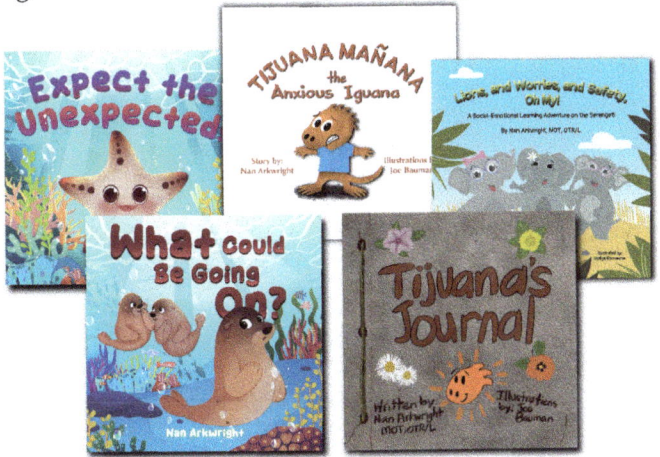

Nan Arkwright, MOT, OTR/L nan.arkwright@gmail.com
www.AHopSkipandaJumpAhead.com/books

www.ingramcontent.com/pod-product-compliance
Lightning Source LLC
Chambersburg PA
CBHW041134120626
46547CB00019B/2984